This is a diary
Written to you

Thank you for taking the time to understand me
I feel like I've been screaming my entire life
But no one's been able to hear my voice

About me:
I'm very relatable
I'm someone like you
I am human
I have a heart
I've been hurt
I've been broken
I know what it feels like
to hide behind everyone else

Thank you, God for allowing me to
Acknowledge my own courage and strength
I transformed myself into a better woman
And realized *I must put together this book*

20/20 Vision

My vision grew when I realized
I am the only one
Who can control how I feel
My vision grew when I realized
You don't get to pick and choose
When you want to be a part of my life
I grew love for myself when I realized
I am capable of standing my own ground
I created a name for myself
Because I am *worth* the title of greatness

It took me awhile to realize
I am the only one who can make myself happy
I am the only one who can accept myself
For who I really am
I didn't need you to tell me I am pretty
I didn't need you to tell me I am smart
For years, I sought validation from people
Who didn't have me in their best interest
I was broken trying to build a foundation
In places that never welcomed me 100%

I wish someone told me about the world
Before the world crushed me
I never understood why genuine people
Are so hard to come across
Why is it hard to be a good person?
I grew up believing everyone had
The same heart, yet everyone did me dirty
They took me for advantage
They took my kindness for weakness
I wanted us to be happy but instead
You had plans of becoming better than me

Beware of the angels
That are really hidden demons
Beware of the smiles
That are waiting to benefit
From your accomplishments
Beware of the company
You allow to step foot in your home
Beware of anyone
Who gets the opportunity
To experience the very best
Version of who you are

I no longer want the pain
I developed from your neglect
Throughout all these years
I've been blind, believing
You were my healer
You built toxins in me
That I'm constantly in battle of removing
But for as long as I fought for my peace again
I realized I found a cure that's better than you;

Myself

Dear self,

You bloomed into this incredible woman
The way you carry yourself
The way you wake up early in the morning
More driven than you were a day before
You remind yourself daily how close you are
To goals you dreamed about your whole life
I am so proud of you
You remain confident in yourself
In your craft and in your creativity
I want to remind you to
Never be too hard on yourself
On days people leave you
Or misunderstand you
Or disappoint you
Because you are a stronger woman
No one is able to define you

Goodbyes

I no longer want you to be a part of my life
I don't crave the attention you use to give me
I don't crave the compliments
I believed were genuine
I don't want your open arms anymore
I don't want your kisses or your hugs
I no longer seek for your approval

I wanted a lot people
To be better for me but
No one ever met my standards
Sometimes I question
My ability to find love again
I always wondered if there was
Someone perfect enough for me
I wondered if my standards were too high
Or if the time just wasn't right
I wonder if I was too selfish
Or if I wasn't selfish enough
Everyone always told me
I'll never find the perfect man
Everyone always told me
To lower my standards
But why do I have to be with someone
Who can't love me fully
Or cherish me how I needed to
Or love me how I was taught to love
I don't need someone
Who can't see how valuable I am
I don't need someone
Who doesn't see how enough I am
I don't need lust, I need love

Dear Men,

I'm tired of explaining myself to you
I'm tired of being someone's property
I'm tired of being a sex object
I'm tired of being ignored
I'm tired of you not caring enough
I'm tired of being a second option
I'm tired of being lied to
I'm tired of you walking away from me
I'm tired of you not taking me seriously
I'm tired of being tired

Reasons Why I Hate You

I always end up loving you
More than you love me
I don't think you ever loved me
To begin with
Was any of it real?

You treat me less than a human being
You continued to hurt me and watch me
Go back to you over and over again
Because you knew
No matter how much pain I receive
I'll always come back to you
Because I loved you

You knew how down I was for you
You knew how vulnerable I was
You knew how desperate I was
To find real love
But you took me for granted

You manipulated my love
You used me
You abandoned me
You allowed me to feel worthless
You allowed me to be numb
You made me lose myself completely

Forever alone

I was so desperate to fill my love tank
From people that had nothing to offer me
I wanted to be more than accepted
But I forgot not everyone is available
I had to learn how to distance myself
From people who were temporary
I didn't know who'd stay or who'd leave
But I learned to appreciate everyone
That once had a chance to stop by

I was too selfish to realize
You could be better without me
Sometimes I forget
There are more lives to live
And I guess more women to feed
Than just myself
For only a short period of time I was happy
But I later found myself miserable
All over again, asking
Why do I keep hurting myself like this?
How can someone who claim to love me
Get up and leave the very next day?
I realized this whole concept of life meant
Everyone is supposed to follow their own path

May I thank you for stopping by

My family made me find love again
I thought I would find love
In a boy or a group of friends
But damn was that a joke
I feel so ashamed for
How many times I put friends over family
How was I so foolish?
All along I've been searching for
Acceptance and love in all the wrong places
But I need to thank God
Because this whole time
I had unconditional love right in front of me

♥

Dear family,

You are the best thing that happened to me
I want to first apologize because for years
I neglected your love
I took everything for granted
Now that I'm older
I wish we had more time together
We weren't always a perfect family but
I realized how perfectly imperfect we are
And that alone satisfies me
Thank you for never leaving me
While I was trying to find myself
I don't know who I would be
Without all the wisdom and knowledge
You fed into my brain
Because of you, I've built character
Thank you for teaching me all of your mistake
There's no way I could've made it alone

To Those I Truly Loved:

I knew I really loved you
When I wanted what was best for you
I wanted you to reach your full potential
With or without me in your life
But can I express how much it hurts
To love someone more
Than they love themselves
How awful it feels
To want more for someone
Who isn't willing to see
How great they can be
I realize not everyone around me
Is interested in my best blessings
I no longer give help to those
Who aren't willing to grow
I can only pray
God helps you see the light
I've been dying to shine on you

Passionate Affection

Let me love you deeply
And see the smile on your face
I want to remind you
No one will ever be able to
Bring you down
Because me by your side
Will always be enough

I want to give what I've been
Dying to grasp my hands on
Because I never got a chance
To experience *real love*
At its purest form

I know real love is something
People are willing to die for
Allow me to recognize reasons
I'd die for you any day

I know real love doesn't leave you
And make you go unnoticed
I want to show you
Passionate affection
For the rest of your life

Let me kiss your
Soft lips with compassion
And remind you how much
I love the attention you give me

I want to remind you
I am more than just
A pleasurable moment
But moments that'll last us
For the rest of eternity

Like a Drug

Addicted to you
Like ol' girl
On white girl
I want to be stuck with you
And live without fear
Because I know with you around
I am safe
You make me feel at home
No matter how far we depart
We'll never be apart from each other
Because together we are whole
You make me feel alive
On days I felt dead
Like when you took me on a trip
And we went skiing for hours
Addicted to you
Like ol' girl
On white girl
Like a drug

I never want to cut you lose

Love

I know I am happy
When I no longer care
When you see my bare skin

You always remind me
How beautiful my skin is
My soul softens
As I learn I can finally
Break down these walls
Of doubts and insecurities

I learn to grow more
For myself than for others
But I want to thank you
Because you brought out
The best in me
On days I doubted myself

I want to show you light
Because you showed me
A path through darkness
And held my hand
On days I couldn't see

I thank you because
Now I am able to breathe
To feel okay
To feel at ease
It's been such a long time
That I felt this pleased

Irreplaceable

What a time to be alive
When the one you love
Loves you back
And you realize one thing
You can never be replaced

What a time to be alive
When you find you can seek
Happiness without trying
God made me realize one thing
You can never be replaced

I found joy by giving
More than I expected to receive
This is something many can't comprehend—
You can never be replaced

As I watch how selfish we want each other
To only ourselves
I want to just remind you
You can never be replaced

As seductive our looks can attract eyes
We don't pay attention to
You need to realize one thing
You can never be replaced

There are days when we are fooled
And run away from our love
But our loyalty still remains in place
You can never be replaced

True Affection

You continue to treat me better
Than the woman I was yesterday
I ask God to show me ways
I can love you more *deeply and sincerely*
I want to show you how passionate I can be
Because I feel as if loyalty and commitment
Isn't enough to make up for
What you do for me on a daily basis
As deep as I am in love with you
I can't imagine life without you
The way you cater to me
And treat me so amazingly effortless
I wonder what I ever did
To deserve someone like you

Signs of Healthy Living

I want to wake up every day
To you singing my favorite songs
While I stir up your favorite meal
Lying beside you, *I am myself*

Alone and together, unbothered
Clouds of love surround our air
As we breathe in the real meaning of life

The way you nurture my soul
The way you caress my body
Without a single touch
You warm me up

Your warmth reminds me
Great things take time
And great things are worth the wait

How beautiful you are
The way you check up on me
And get defensive anytime
Someone tries to disrespect my name

I love how much you want
To protect me and my happiness
To protect me and my peace

How lucky I am to be able to call you mine

To all my best friends:

I hope one day you're able to find someone
Who can love you as much as I genuinely do
How much I adore listening to your problems
And seeing you grow and become a better you
How much I love taking you on lunch dates
And rewarding you for your accomplishments
I love the way you carry yourself
I love watching you bloom
I love listening to your goals
And seeing them turn into reality

To all my best friends,
I thank you for always being
More than just a friend
But more as a sister or a brother
A family member I never want to be away from
I thank you for adding so much value to my life
And laughers I never want to discontinue
For all the memories we've made
And the times you stayed by my side
And never judged me
I am reminded how grateful I am
To have you in my life

To all my best friends,
Thank you for teaching me
What real friends are
And thank you for teaching me
What real friends aren't
I trusted you with my problems
And you gave me strength
I relied on your answers
So you told me the truth

You always told me what I needed to hear
Instead of words that only gave me comfort
You reminded me of bravery and how
I am able to conquer anything
That comes along my way
You remind me the views I should take upon life
And how beautiful life already is
Regardless of the situations I'm in
Thank you for allowing me
To see a better perspective on life

Thank you for being my friend
- Yamilah

A Letter to Mom:

How amazing you are
On days you continue to nurture me
Even when I entered adulthood—
You're still by my side
You gave me blessings
And prayed on my behalf
Against any type of evil
I may stumble across
I want to thank you
For your gratitude and strength
You manage to show how
Strong mothers really are
When days become tough and
Anxiety still doesn't overrule you
How amazing you are
To work without acknowledgment
To give without receiving
To love when clouds are gray and
Men become astray
I know I could I always come back to you
Thank you for everything, mom
Thank you for setting an example
 Of whom I wish to become

Dear Dad,

You weren't always perfect
But I still love you till this day
I forgive you for not being there
When I needed you
I forgive you for when
Mom needed you the most
I forgive you for not understanding
The importance of a father figure
I still don't know who
Made you who you are
But I'll continue to be your daughter
Because I know deep down
You need me
And I know deep down
I still need you

I love you, dad

Worst Pain in The World

When you told my mom she was worthless
I felt as if you were also speaking to me
Every word you spoke to her
Every piece of pain you gave my mom
I also felt and it broke me
You forgot my mom was also human
You forgot that she needed love
I never felt pain that was so real

The Worst Part

There were many nights that I cried
Because I just couldn't believe
How broken my family was
My mom was amazing at hiding her pain
I think that's where I get it from
I didn't think she was someone
That could ever stumble
I never knew how she felt
Until she told me when I got older
When my mom told me, she was depressed
I became depressed
My heart shattered

When you are raised
By a holy woman
It changes you
It changes how you think
It changes how you love

When you love someone
You become vulnerable towards them
You become protective over them
Their emotions become yours
Their love become yours

I'd do anything to see you smile

Confessions

I have to admit
I've had disappointing days
For not doing enough
Like the perfectionists
That are idolized on
Social media platforms
I have to admit to
Social depression
Because of the newsfeed
Of my peers doing better than I am
I sat here in the same spot
Contemplating on my worth and
Meaning of existence
It's been a long journey
Of constant doubt and disbelief

For a long time
I've been in competition
With everyone around me
It seemed like all the pretty girls
Were more valuable on the internet
I wanted to become one of them
As I put on more makeup everyday
And wore clothes that showed off my curves
I realized how much more attention I got
More people wanted to be my friend
More people were interested in me

I never realized how fake the world was until now.

It made me happy yet
So insecure on the inside
I couldn't go anywhere
Without a pair of lashes
I couldn't leave my house
Without foundation on my face
I felt the need to
Hide my true identity
From the rest of the world
Being pretty set expectations
Towards reality that wasn't real
The prettier I got
The faker things felt and
The shadier people became
Life was unrealistic
I got so caught up in being
The perfect barbie
I neglected who I really was and
Fabricated my true identity

Things That Are Important to Me

    1.) <u>Family</u>
I didn't realize the importance of family
Until everyone else left me
I question if I'm worthy enough
Of a family that continues to take me back
Regardless of how many mistakes I've made
I'm grateful because I know
Not everyone has a family to come home to
I want to thank my mom for always providing for me
I want to thank my dad for always making me laugh
I want to thank my sister for being a good role model
I want to thank my grandma for being there when I
least expected her to

    2.) <u>Real Friends</u>
Having friends is fun but having
Real friends changed my life
I didn't realize the importance of real friends
Until one day I became broke
And only my real friends had my back
I didn't realize the importance of real friends
Until I experience my first heartbreak
And only my real friends stood by my side
Real friends are the ones you go to
When you suffer and need a hug
Real friends are the ones you go to
When you want to get away from reality
Real friends are the ones you go to

When you need a laugh or a shoulder to cry one
All at once, real friends don't leave you
When you have nothing left to offer
Real friends offer you everything

3.) <u>Respect, Honesty, Trust</u>
As I got older I realized
Character plays a big role
And when I think of character
I think of respect, honesty and trust
Respect is given
But real respect is *earned*
Through honesty and trust
I was able to build amazing allies
That I know I could always depend on
I realized the importance of this
In every human being
I appreciate everyone
That was able to provide me
With respect, honesty and trust

Thank you

4.) <u>God</u>
I've been lost for years
Because I forgot about God
I've made too many mistakes
Not realizing
God could of guided me
I had so many doubts and insecurities
Failures and meltdowns
All that could of been prevented
If I realized Gods always here

Dear God,

I never want to lose sight of you again.

Dear Me,

I can't apologize to myself enough
For abandoning my own worth

How amazing I already am
With the color of my skin
To the way that I laugh
Or the wisdom that I speak

I'm sorry for allowing others
To come in before
Me and my own happiness
I now find ways to protect my peace

I no longer seek peace
From anyone who'll fuck me over
And burden my soul

I'll acknowledge my physical and mental health
I'll always be worthy of smiles and bundles of joy
And people who don't see me as a second option

It's time I love myself entirely

I apologize for all those days I left myself
I promise to be great again
I promise to always put myself first

Deep Dark Secrets

The Truth

I hid my pain because
I was too ashamed to speak on it
I was too afraid of how people would react
I was too in shock that
This actually happened to me
I secretly blamed myself for this incident
Maybe I should of never had sex
Maybe I should of never
Allowed you to become too aggressive
Maybe I was just... dumb?
My mind haunts me of how many times
I screamed for you to stop
But you continued to push yourself inside me
My hands were held behind my back
Leaving me in the most unhelpful position
This was the moment that changed my life forever
I never knew that in a million years
You would hurt me in this way
You robbed me from my innocence and my peace
You left me so confused in that bathroom stall
I finally began to ask myself *who am I to you?*
Is this really what I was worth?

I've been traumatized for years
By someone who claimed to love me
I've been blinded by love
How was I so stupid?

What you've done to me was
Nothing near normal or okay
You left a scar on me that
I'll never be comfortable enough
Sharing with the rest of the world
You killed a happy soul that
Was once so eager to love
You made me feel so foolish...
I was too hurt to face the truth
That you actually raped me
I couldn't believe it

I didn't

Benign Tumor

I couldn't believe the words that
Came out of my doctor's mouth
I couldn't believe the causes
when I Googled benign tumor
You were the reason behind
My depression and my trauma
My triggers and nightmares
All of this PTSD
You did this to me

I no longer crave love
From another individual
I no longer crave intimacy
I no longer crave sex
I only fear the abuse
That will re-haunt me
If I try to go back
And find love again

I've been afraid

I don't want to learn anyone else
I don't want to learn this love word anymore
I came to the conclusion that
This type of trauma
Will never be able to leave me
It's been over a decade and
You're still here haunting my well-being

Waiting Until Marriage

I came to the conclusion
That there is no boy out here
Who is worth opening my legs to
I no longer feel comfortable
With the idea of sex
Nor do I have the urge
To want anything intimate

Day of surgery

When I got my tumor removed
I felt like weights been lifted off my shoulder
I finally defeated something
I felt good about myself
I had tears of relief this day but also
Tears from my trauma
I couldn't explain how I felt
But I knew I was sad
I was anxious
I was overwhelmed
My tumor was removed
But my PTSD grew
This surgery reopened wounds
I tried my best to hide

I began to hate myself
And my experiences
I asked God, why me?
Why do I have to explain
To guys I get intimate with
That I got raped?
Why do I have to tell someone
To keep things gentle with me
Because I have PTSD?
Why am I so triggered?

I was a deeply shamed woman
I put myself down for nearly everything
I couldn't stand looking at myself in the mirror
I tried my best to move forward
But it only made things worse
Sooner than later, I became depressed
Desperately seeking a therapist
But too afraid of taking the first step
Desperately seeking attention
But too afraid of owning up to my truth

I needed healing
I needed someone
Anyone to love me again

Relationship Goals?

I was never the women
You wanted to be with
It was only parts of us
You fell in love with
But it wasn't me
You loved the idea
Of what we were
You loved the idea
That we could be something great
But you never really liked me
You didn't acknowledge
The things that I took pride in
You didn't take the time to
Understand my emotions
You didn't even know
What my passions were
You never paid attention to
The small bits of me
That made me who I am
You just fell in love
With the idea of us

Night of February 19, 2020

I lost myself
I didn't realize how important mental health was
Until I had no control over my body
I got tired of this routine
Aren't you guys tired of this too?
But I wanted to be a regular girl this day
Hang out, catch a vibe, have great sex
I was so excited to catch a good vibe
I was so excited to have a sex life again
I remember telling my homegirls about it
I remember them cheering me on (lol)
But that was the opposite of how my night went
The moment I tried to have sex with him
My flashbacks hit me
I felt as if you raped me all over again
I felt so shameful
I was so mad at myself
I couldn't help but put myself down
Why couldn't this fucking end?

After bursting into tears
I immediately put my clothes back on
I was so embarrassed that night
I didn't talk to him again

Panic Attacks

Once I left, that's when my panic attack began
I had no control over myself
I couldn't stop my heavy breathing
I couldn't stop my anxiety
I felt anxious driving all the way home
My body was shaking
My heart was pounding
I screamed to the top of my lungs
My eyes were swollen from crying
I almost forced myself in a car crash
Everyone looked at me crazy

I went through weeks of hell
And depression all over again
Once I thought I overcame something
I knew again that I played myself
I was so eager to move forward
But I always forget
Healing doesn't happen overnight
I decided to allow myself to breathe
And gave me reminders that
Everything will be okay

I watched everyone else live
A beautiful romance
As I sat here hopeless
Triggered, and lonely

Typical Tuesdays

The more I liked someone
And they leave me
The more I wanted a replacement
I needed to find someone new
And it needed to happen fast

It became a ritual
We'd talk, have sex
He'd leave me, I'd get hurt
I'd find a replacement
It became a bad habit of mine

I would repeat this process
Over and over again
Not realizing how much damage
I'm bringing to my soul

But the more I repeated this
The more I realized
How less I felt each time

As each person left me
I felt as if a part of me
Left with them too
And in the end I realized
How *empty* I felt being alone

I couldn't take it
I needed someone there for me
I needed love
Desperately
Anyone, who can show me
There's someone worth loving
Worth being with
Worth laughing with

Dear Depression,

You were like a season to me
Every year I would see you
During the holidays
Especially on my birthday month

It became a tradition
To just wake up and hate myself
I didn't want to eat
I didn't want to socialize
I found comfort hiding in my bedroom
I enjoyed knowing people couldn't see
How sad I really was

For years I've been covering for you
You were so toxic to me
But for some reason I loved it
I couldn't find myself away
From you for too long

I couldn't understand
My urge for negativity
Yet I made no efforts
In finding a solution

No matter how much we fought
You always won every battle
Just like everyone else in my life
You always got up
And left whenever you pleased

You got to the best of me
You were the reason why I hated myself

Suicidal Thoughts

There came a point in my life
Where my self-hate reflected to suicidal thoughts
I had too many days where
I wanted to kill myself
I had three days where I tried to kill myself
I didn't have enough motivation to stay here
I didn't have enough people that loved me
I didn't have anyone that really cared about me
I wished death upon myself too many times
I just wanted everything to end

My Reflection

This whole time I believed
Patience was my enemy
I ran from it
I avoided it
I acted as if patience didn't exist
When I encountered pain
I wanted to heal immediately
Move forward
Start a new beginning
Meet new people
I realized things never work out
How I want them to
Because it was God's story
I needed to follow
I didn't need to create
Anything that wasn't there
What's meant for me
Would happen naturally
I didn't need to force love
When in reality
Real love is never forced

It was hard dealing with
Depression on my own
I reached my lowest point in life
To where I wanted to end it
But truth is now,
I am a new person
A healthy one
A happy one
I now look back and
Pat the old me on the back
I've dealt with pain
The best way I could
Now it's time I help others

My Realizations

It took me a long time to realize
I'm the only person who can heal myself
Even if I waited for company
I would only be satisfied
By someone else's comfort
Spending so much time alone
I realized that patience wasn't my
Enemy anymore but my friend
The only way I overcame my very own emotions
Was facing the fact that healing requires patience

Dear Patience,

It's so hard to be with you
And stay by your side
You are easier said than done
I still hate you
But I love you at the same time
They always tell you to
Face your biggest fears
I think you're who I fear the most
I trouble with "what-if's" and rejection
I trouble with fear and the unknown
What will be the outcome?
What if I fail? What if I regret?
But with you, Patience
You taught me to be calm
To be fearless, and to be at peace
You taught me to
Have faith in my process
For so long, I've struggled with you
But now I thank you
Because today, *I am a changed women*

Independent Women

I can only thank God for saving me
He knew the type of man you were
And I was blind to think
You were my healer
I was blind to believe
I needed anyone by my side
I was blind to believe
I alone, wasn't enough
I now stand high
On my own two feet
I now practice self-love
I practice happiness through isolation
I practice being alone
I practice independency
I never felt so happy
And so loved by me
No one else could give me
This feelings of satisfaction

When you build
A relationship with God
You begin to feel free
You will no longer feel
The need to lie or cheat
You won't need to
Prove anything to anyone
You'll become true to yourself because
You want to be true to God
When everyone else fails you
Keep praying and talk to God
When life becomes rewarding
Keep praying and talk to God

♥

I accepted everything
God handed over to me
And I don't question his decisions
Everything I overcame
Made me into a stronger woman

Happiness is a choice
I must *always* say yes to

A letter to you:

I am praying on your behalf
For your greatness
For your prosperity
For your happiness

I hope one day
You can feel rich without money
Be rich without trying
Be rich with no force

I pray you find those
Who are built on love
And surround yourself with people
Who are able to uplift
Your mind, spirit, and soul

I hope you avoid people
Who constantly break you down
You deserve to be uplifted every single day
You deserve to feel good about yourself

I hope you have the courage to
Accept people for leaving you
I hope you can carry enough strength
To leave toxic people behind

I hope you are able to pray
For those who have wronged you
I hope you can forgive people
Who threw dirt on your name

You are a leader, not a follower
You have a lot of potential
You have the ability to grow

I hope you find people
Who can see how amazing you are
I hope you find people
Who remind you of your strengths

When you feel alone,
I promise those are just emotions
You've always been enough
With no one by your side

Continue to love
Continue to flourish
Continue to practice self-love
Continue to carry high vibrations

When you decide to see the brighter side of life
You will find true happiness
You will understand love in a selfish world

When you learn to live a life on love
Everything becomes beautiful

Enjoyed my book?

Contact me and let me know what you think.

Email: yamilahnguyen@gmail.com
IG & Twitter: @yamilahn_
PO BOX #88772 Tukwila WA, 98138